A Color Called Harvest

poems by

Faith Paulsen

Finishing Line Press
Georgetown, Kentucky

A Color Called Harvest

ACKNOWLEDGMENTS

Whether the bird, Blast Furnace: http://www.blastfurnacepress.
com/2013_04_01_archive.html
Home is where, Sprout: http://www.persistentgreen.com/2013/10/sprout-24-
now-available-gratitude-issue.html
Time Signature, Working Late, When Women Waken: www.whenwomenwaken.
org (website currently being reconstructed)
Holy Sonnet, Milk Lets, Still Here, MOON Magazine: http://moonmagazine.org/
faith-paulsen-three-poems-2015-03-01/
In the red wine café, *In Gilded Frame*, ed. A.J. Huffman and April Salzano, 2013,
Kind of a Hurricane Press
Written in the Palm of My Hand, *Three Minus One: Stories of Parents' Loss and
Love*, ed. Sean Hanish & Brooke Warner, 2014, She Writes Press
You can put, Front Porch Review: http://frontporchrvw.com/issue/october-2015/
article/you-can-put

Publisher: Leah Maines

Editor: Christen Kincaid

Cover Art: Photo by Faith Paulsen

Author Photo: Paz Paulsen-Sacks, Spoken Word Istanbul

Cover Design: Elizabeth Maines

Printed in the USA on acid-free paper.
Order online: www.finishinglinepress.com
also available on amazon.com

Author inquiries and mail orders:
Finishing Line Press
P. O. Box 1626
Georgetown, Kentucky 40324
U. S. A.

Table of Contents

Still There 1

Ode to a Flatfish 2

Elegy for Yellow Paint 3

Spring Peepers 4

Funerary Portrait of a Couple, 7th Century BCE 5

Low Music 6

Milk lets 8

Our shared skin 9

Whether the bird 10

In the Red Wine Café 11

Written on the Palm of My Hand 12

You can put 13

Time Signature 14

Wall Décor 15

Au Revoir 17

Working Late 19

We speak, knowing 20

The End of the Visit 21

Holy Sonnet 22

Home is where 23

Song 24

Pepper 25

For Barton, Paz, Seth and Gideon,
and for my parents,
with all my love

Still There

Inspired by a painting by Elizabeth Catanese

After class, two children
clean the blackboard erasers,
bumping them together, soft cymbals.
White dust billows, settles on eyes and noses.
They laugh, choking, play teacher,
white chalk tapping. In a game of hangman,
letter by letter, two words assemble,
a school play, brave, vulnerable,
Still There. Once you've seen the words
on the cover, you don't need
to read the book. The practice
is love. The dreaming pupils, blank slates,
play catch with the erasers.
The girl, over-excited, hardballs hers,
straight at the surface
bulls-eye.
But instead of hitting the board,
the eraser escapes—
a gap in space—
leaving a spray of sugar on open lips,
the sacred text a smudge.

Ode to a Flatfish

Bilateral
symmetrical
hatchling, you
paddle impossibly
vertical a reed uprooted
one eye on each side. Daring
to skim heady altitude skittering
up to tickle the skin of air un-
breathable. When left and right
eyes observe nothing in common,
how many dimensions do you see?
You grow from larval to juvenile.
Bone and cartilage stiffen, nerves
ripen. Tides take you, gravity pulls.
You submarine to shadowed water,
you put away childish things. Weight
of water presses and turns you.
The eye on the underside migrates
to the topside until you look up
always. A different point
of view. Sinking, you are
translated. You spread
your lop-sided self
like melted butter
on the bottom of a pan.
Last chance to flap
and flail.
Now dig in.
You wait half-
buried to chew
other fishes' spawn.
Carpet with eyes
open, use them both
to look up. You
flounder.

Elegy for Yellow Paint

Sun-aged now, flattened like soil
pressed under fifteen years
of school-morning complaints,
picture books, the breath
of the night, dripping
like watercolor in rain,
running into the hue
once chosen for its disposition,
now a dry cornstalk
under my hand.

Pigment like butter
on the telescope wand,
the roller crackling,
erases the yellow, overtakes
with crisp scent and hue,
tearing away from itself
a bright rip, clean,
semi-gloss,
a color called harvest,
orange-skin surface.

Today, on the freshly-painted wall
standing back,
gathering in, I notice,
bleeding through years-old
yellow touch-ups,
persistent as vines from soil,
black marker scrawls
the first three letters of a kindergartener's name.

Spring Peepers

In the ice-armored, ice-crackled night
I stop, back up. I rethink admonitions.
To your sleeping ear, folded lid,
I storybook
infuse cold night with
the preposterous population of spring.
Even now, sleeper, I lullaby,
the woodfrog deep in leaf litter, heartstopped,
anti-freeze pumped
good frog hibernates. He is made in waiting.
He knows he will know spring by the rise
of temperature, of blood. Red-eyed
spotted clawed Sherlock toad
interprets the cues, deduces,
hears heartbeat reveille,
It's time to defrost. Time
for spring rains and vernal pools.
Breathing through skin
in moist night green Pacman frog
recognizes food by its movement,
the cricket
tongue-flipped mouth-popped.
The singing rises,
Balloon-throated chorus frog
preep-peeps whistle-chirps. Rain brings
restlessness. Firebellied gladiator
whipping frog belts it out,
O Sole Mio—while ear-perked
the enraptured listener frog lifts,
tunes herself, homes in, drawn
by song. She asks,
Am I getting warmer?
My tadpole, on this winter night,
may your dreams be populated,
a Hallelujah Chorus of frogs.

Funerary portrait of a couple, 7th century BCE

You and I enter the wide gallery,
our contrasting art-appreciation styles,
my inwardness, your need to entertain,
our duet, my flute to your piano.
Two polished marble faces greet us dead-on,
reclining Roman-style.

Their elbows lift them from elegant pillows,
upright, animated,
his arm a presence on her shoulder.
He turns to her, perhaps to tell a story.
Two smiles curve, echoes of her breasts.
She has heard many times
the story he's telling,
listens anyhow, smiles,
her gestures warming stone.

Do you think they were
buried together?
You make a joke,
their shared sarcophagus,
while music plays
on the skin of rounded grapes,
pomegranates and olives, a banquet
in the afterlife. Still playfully
she twists one braid
between her fingers.

Low Music

*According to Katy Payne, Acoustic Biologist, elephants communicate
with each other by means of sounds too low and deep for humans
to hear. "The whole herd... will sometimes be still, completely still.
And it's not just a stillness of voice; it's a stillness of body... They're
listening."*

The air around her
throbs, shudders, a thunder
felt in the bones and tusks,
a bass aria deep in the earth.

She leads, the matriarch,
her body a hull
sailing forests of orchids,
between years of walking.
Her steps swim the landscape. She hears,
infrasound,
the youngest calf calling to his mother,
hears her sister comforting him,
thrum, thrum,
thrum. To her,
vibrato means morning,
shudder means night, rumble
the exuberance of abundant water.

Last season, far from the swamp,
a yearling died. Too thin, his song
feeble, he slowed. One knee,
then the other buckled,
went down.
All that day and the next,
the others hauled the body,
trunks scrabbling to grasp.
Finally he fell, a thud that rang
as the herd continued.

This season's migration,
they found the spot,
came upon the staves
of the yearling's carcass.
They halted, throbbing.
Then one by one, we nuzzled the bones,
scent and touch reaching to full length,
lightly fingering
the desert skin,
the skull bowl,
the tuft of hair.

This morning, the herd moves
under rubber tree and kapok,
strangler fig and tulip tree.
She hears a note—
Movement stops.
A common vibration stills
all throats, holds hooves in place.

Her ears unfold.
She bores down,
down into deep sound.

Milk lets

down, hearing your voices,
rivers, rainfall, underground
springs, want to spill
out of me into you, my flavor
on your breath, each of you
my only, my heart curled
around the space where you
used to be.

Bending, I place you,
your clean, untried feet on the sand,
right, left. One day,
you surprise, hold your weight—
the next you run—and I stop
breathing, dissolve into
salt and sound. My ocean,
red sun and wind rush up
to wash and
test you as you venture
further down the strand.
I ride your footprints like
the waves.

Use what I gave you, while,
uncounted departures later,
I wait here still,
watching, biting my lip.

Our shared skin

sheds droplets.
Soles settle on tile, surprised
to find wetness, sliding into, fear,
adrenalin—heels suspend for a moment—
the toes grip, prevent disaster.
Heedless steps convey her
from bathroom to bedroom to
closet door. She doesn't even notice
how I've saved her.

Between closet and mirror, she suffers
as always, her ceramic hardness turned on
our nakedness even as my processes continue
In her service—air and fluids pump,
digest, shelter, the valiant
membranes, choreography well-rehearsed.
In all my power, she sees only faults,
blames me for shapes that interrupt the lines.

I speak to her in sensations, in lightness
and weight, what I need and don't need,
what is enough and whole.
Unhearing she hurries toward the bedroom door, grabbing
her keys. As she ignores,
my senses surround her, they taste and see
only for her.

Why do you hate me,
all my cells want to plead, when I pour out
everything I have
to prevent you from falling? Please,
my symbiont,
inhere with me.

Whether the bird

slammed into the picture window, or
was found in the grass behind the house, or
was killed with a BB gun
or rock, however its warm body cooled,
here it is now,
an object,
each of its wingtips held
between a thumb and forefinger
of this eleven-year-old boy.
The blue jay's wings stretch upward,
toward the overcast sky,
striated feathers fanned,
its head almost touching
the child's dry cheek,
its body a pendant.

In the wine red café

On a street of rowhouses,
this one storefront floats above
the foundation. You can feel on your skin
the silver thread
that stitches the room together.
Speak up, I can't hear you,
over the spinning music.
The bartender's crowd arrives
just for his shift. They follow him
on Facebook. *Trust me*, he promises,
to curate your experience, and he repeats
our orders from memory.
Music, curly-haired like the woman
at the table, dark-eyed like the man,
bangs out a tune made of
fiddle and harp. A 60-year-old former dancer
plays the tambourine. Laughter
balloons from the table to our left.
The waitress pretends to smile with them.
In the hubbub of conversation,
voices, words build upon each other
like clay vessels like wine bottles
clattered one on top of
the other, teetering,
a leaning tower.
A backbone shifts
in the dark hiding
that crevice, the ribcage.
A table set for four
remains untouched.
Holiness rings in the glass that clinks
and the one that breaks.
You and I share a table,
swimming in red wine, wrapped in
poppy sound,
our centerpiece the silence
in the matrix our hands.

Written on the Palm of My Hand

Years later, across a table
at a charity fundraiser, an Indian palmist
cradles, dips my hand
in water, towels it dry.
At the corners of his eyes, no older than mine,
lines crease and uncrease.
He describes the palmists' map: *Mount of Mercury,*
Father, Mother, upper Mars, health,
longevity, continuation
of the progeny. His finger traces
folds that curl around my thumb, lines
I've never noticed before.
And there it is, my private
truth, woven into the geography of my body,
a birthmark.
He counts, *Lines of Children,*
three strong,
two
weak.

You can put

your hand inside this
absence. The half-set table, knife, cup,
saucer. Lunch is suspended,
undone. The chair, moved, for
some purpose, has not been returned
to its place. From the nine-paned window,
the cold sun slants in. Outside,
on the frozen grass,
beyond the sentinel fencepost,
a splintered log. Here,
the plain white plate,
cold to the touch,
lifts up its porcelain hope.

Time signature

The spoon tips
into my father's slack mouth—his
last taste, French Silk ice cream.
For days after, he stays,
unmoving except for his breath and his
long musician's fingers spread out on the sheet's
silent keyboard. We gather, sit, watch snowflakes
settle on the glass, inches from
the houseplant at his bedside. Everything my father
ever did or was
lingers vaporous
in this room. In memory I sit next to him
on the organ bench, my job
to follow the sheet music, to anticipate his
quick eyes always four bars ahead.
I'm entrusted to know when
to turn the page. Instead, I look down
as his thumb on middle-C slides
under his index finger, letting go of one key
to take its turn on the next, holding
the long note—the note, he'd told me,
was a star—while his hand fills in
a new chord.

Wall Decor

Let's keep only
the things we love. This painting
the color of red clay, spattered circles
rose and aqua. I want to put my hands into it.
Look at the variety
of textures. We have to keep
the ceramic wall pocket—If we kept
everything our kids made, there'd be no room
for us—Each piece you own
has a history. In what room
do you tell your stories?
I love the way the color picks up
the blue trim, the thread
in the rug. This artist
is a genius. Yeah, it's me.

Wait—I know it's blasphemy but—How
would you feel
about hanging this painting
the other way? No, no, never.
Well, it does
work.

Think about
placement. The bold colors work well
here but this one is more muted.
Think of the way you flow
through your house.
What do you want to see at the top
of the stairs? What belongs
over the mantel? This piece
would be wasted on that wall.

If we hang the lute
here, its lines are echoed
in the lines
of the corner cabinet.
Dr Albert Barnes
would be proud.
Did we always
have that mobile?
Think about margins,
negative space. It's like a maze
your eyes can solve.

Let me ask you—How do you feel about
asymmetry?

Au Revoir

It will be alright. The airplane
will snowflake down
onto the pillowed runway
at your destination.
Someone will be waiting at the gate
waving your name.
Someone trustworthy.
There will be a job and a bed
and infallible cellphone reception.

If you snorkel, the Pacific will open
like an oystershell, empty
of stingrays, without undertow,
storm-free and blue
as your bedroom walls.
If you cut your foot on the coral reef,
you will seek immediate medical attention.

If you crawl on hands and knees
through a water-filled cave, you will do so
sober, enlightened,
and you will emerge
blinking into noonday light.

It will be alright. If, as you sleep,
a scorpion scuttles across
your sun-brown hand,
you will be immune to its sting.
When you turn your head
to look at the sky,
the muscles in your neck
will glide into place. When you take photos
of the village children, they will beam
into their own unfamiliar faces,

and when you call me,
as you will do every week,
you will tell me stories of keys without doors
and I will listen,
gleaming.

You will bebop on top of the volcano and not
burn your feet. You will swan dive
from the high rock cliff
and not make a splash.

Working Late

At the desk, I eat a sandwich, a bruised
apple. I sip from a coffee mug
and read across its side
the insignia of an elementary school, now
closed, its playground empty.
The office chair swivels,
my hips turn, legs bend, one then
the other. On the wall
there is a picture
hook, a backstory. Outside the
building a scratching, later, a siren—
and at last, my own
need tolls. I want
them back, the rounded minutes,
the used cherry desk we called
"antique," the spontaneous
walks for late-night
milkshakes, my
father, my child, the blue heron lifting
off the creek, *I want them back*,
the plastic laundry basket we used
for a bassinet, the life
I bled away. I stand up,
reach. Life throbs
in the missing parts.

We speak, knowing

the other won't hear
until a second later.
I call you at night,
make the calculation,
my time to yours—convert AM to PM, then add four.
You answer eight thousand miles away, where it is
tomorrow morning. Time-lapsed, time-
shifted—our words stumble and interrupt.
—*So glad to hear*—
—*I wanted to tell you*—
Air-mail packages hover mid-journey: Tea, spices,
macaroni and cheese—non-perishable gifts that fit
in a box—lose their way en route to Malekula,
(*Bali Hai*, said Rogers and Hammerstein,
pain in the ass, said Captain Cook),
your *Melanesian* island of pineapples and orchids.
—*Did you get the*—
—*Thank you for the*—
All we've ever had
is a point of
intersection, a thin place where time overlaps.
At home, I stand on one leg, arms twisted,
until you return. The pose requires
constant adjustment. I stay anyhow. —*Are you?*—
—*Did they?*—
—*We're all together, here*, you answer,
your voice wide-eyed.
A picture I will see later:
You and your brothers,
ankle-deep in soft volcanic ash.
I want to say, but you already know:
Inhabit your body.
Spend your whole life.

The End of the Visit

You feel the vibration
in the zip of the dufflebag,
the search for misplaced socks,
steps on the staircase,
the hoof beats of its approach.
The parting is coming.
You so dread that time
you almost want it over
but then their concrete absence
will move in with you
to stay.

Then it arrives—the moment
opens the door.
You rush into its arms.
You try too hard to say everything,
memorize everything
pack everything you can
into a suitcase or a hug.
You never want the goodbye to pass
but it does,
clip clopping away
diminishing like a sound.

Except they take you with them,
the residue of your hair and cells
dusted on the loved ones' skin.

And they always leave something behind,
a toothbrush,
a book left face-down on the nightstand.
You will pick it up
and hold it,
the broken jar of your convergence,
a shard you will spend hours
examining.

Holy Sonnet
A Response to John Donne

God does not want to batter your heart
force to break, blow, burn or overthrow,
despite your prayers to overtake by power.
Fractured, mistaken, you feebly block the door
against the approaching light, the knock—
of the paramedic, and not an enemy.
While you thrash, your physician by love grown
cosmographer throws open GPS and first aid kit,
strong hand presses on your ribcage, breath blows in
to your nostrils, God's taste on your splintered lips,
your body a map, this your south-west discovery—
Though you may beg, John Donne, God
open-handed, frees your will to bend.
She knocks, breathes, shines and seeks to mend.

Home is where

in the kitchen you chop a yellow onion,
the cold water running, so that
your eyes don't burn.

over the desk, saved, like a fly in amber,
the red paper heart clings to a doily
with dried and crumbling glue.

you no longer notice the upholstery has
receded like a hairline, the wooden step
bowed where feet have passed.

you look out at dogwood leaves
and beyond them, the
woodcut moon.

space between the walls,
mussel shell inside the body, yawning,
balanced on the empty air.

the knife cuts, cross-sections the melon,
a shell, a cranium split into slices
of multi-colored millefiore glass.

the cantaloupe falls open, a geode.
your tongue picks up
sweet juice on lips and chin.

Song

"Welcome is every organ and attribute of me." —*Walt Whitman*

Welcome, legs that sprint,
that convey me
or make me passenger
in invented vehicles that drive, cycle, fly.
Welcome to my stem-like spine,
an armature to yoga-pose my limbs.
Welcome keyboarding wrists
puppet hands and fingers.
Kidneys, welcome as sunshower
or baptism, sweet energetic hormones,
blessed abdomen and groin.
Backs of the shoulders, welcome,
let wind graze and sunlight leave
its blush. Welcome to my laughter
that rises from below my navel,
up to the follicles of my hair.
Welcome to my own brain, left and right,
old brain and neocortex.
To the churning ventricles
called heart chambers
most metaphorical of organs, welcome.
Welcome to scars
of injuries, love and childbirth,
to weak ankle and bad shoulder
and to the fat well-earned by enjoyment.
Welcome bare feet on grass at night.
Eyes, lift up and sing your welcome
while the sky opens its landscape.
You are welcome, throat, to sing
the song of this body, this night.

Pepper

I twist the mill
to break the shell
hear the crack
of dried berry
the oil released
citrus and wood.
Black powder scatters like ash
across my plate.
The humble mix:
Malabar for weight and taste, Sumatra for color,
Penang for strength. Piperine,
the source of spicy taste—
Even its price is
volatile. Once ground its aroma
fades, a rung bell. My nose itches alert
as a startled bird. The back
of the throat puckers
energized to the pores. If I could
I'd pepper
it all.

Faith Paulsen's work has appeared in a variety of journals and collections including *Musehouse Journal,* edited by Kathleen Sheeder Bonnano and David Bonnano, *Apiary, Blast Furnace, Cahoodaloodaling, Front Porch Review, Literary Mama, MOON, Mused, Stoneboat, When Women Waken, Wild River Review.* Her poem "Star Dust" was Honorable Mention in the *Philadelphia Inquirer* Poetry Contest in 2010. Her work has been named Honorable Mention in *Glimmer Train's* Short Story Contest for New Writers in 2006 and has been nominated for a Pushcart. As a high school student, Faith had the honor of studying with Denise Levertov. She received her Bachelor's from Barnard College and her Master's in English Literature from Bryn Mawr. Recent mentors in poetry and prose include Rachel Simon, Amy Small-McKinney and Leonard Gontarek. She lives with her husband and three cats in a house full of books and file folders just outside of Philadelphia, Pennsylvania. She has three sons on three different continents. You can check out her cool new website by TekPoet at faithpaulsen.com. This is her first chapbook.